LIFE IN A MEDIEVAL CITY

LIFE IN A MEDIEVAL CITY

Edwin Benson

WAKING LION PRESS

ISBN 1-60096-064-2

Published by Waking Lion Press, an imprint of The Editorium

The views expressed in this book are the responsibility of the author and do not necessarily represent the position of The Editorium. The reader alone is responsible for the use of any ideas or information provided by this book.

Additions to original text © 2006 by The Editorium. All rights reserved. Waking Lion Press™, the Waking Lion Press logo, and The Editorium™ are trademarks of The Editorium, LLC

The Editorium, LLC
West Valley City, UT 84128-3917
wakinglionpress.com
wakinglion@editorium.com

Contents

Introduction   1

Important Factors Affecting the History of York   3
Geographical Position   3
Military Value of Its Position   4
Political Importance   4

The Places in the City   6
General Appearance   6
Streets   8
Buildings   10
York As a Port   22

Everyday Life in the City   23
Civic Life   23
Parliamentary and National Life   28
Business Life   31
Religious Life   39
Education   48
Entertainments   52
Classes   55

Conclusion   59

Chapter 1

INTRODUCTION

In English history the fifteenth century is the last of the centuries that form the Middle Ages, which were preceded by the age of racial settlement and followed by that of the great Renaissance. Although the active beginnings of this new era are to be observed in the fifteenth century, yet this century belongs essentially to the Middle Ages.

Perhaps the most attractive feature of the Middle Ages is that they were so intensely human. A naive spirit appears in their formal literature, as in Chaucer's account of the Canterbury pilgrims, in their decorated religious manuscripts, in their thought, and very characteristically, in their architecture, which combines a simple naturalness with a bold and daring ingenuity. From columns, the constructional motive of which is so simple and natural, and walls pierced with windows, they erected systems of lofty arches and high stone-vaulted roofs, the stability of which depended on very skilled balancing of thrust and counter-thrust.

Today mediaeval buildings are to be found all over England. The majority of them are examples of an architecture that has not been surpassed for majesty, beauty, size, and constructional skill. Such buildings, without the help of the literary and other memorials, testify by themselves to the greatness of the Middle Ages.

Through the fifteenth century England continued to be in a state of political unrest. There were wars and risings both abroad and at home, for besides the Hundred Years' War (1337–1453) and the Wars of the Roses (1455–1485) there were wars with the Welsh and the Scots, as well as disorders made by powerful, intriguing barons. The barons and great landowners took advantage of the weak royal rule to increase their own power. Parliament, especially the House of Commons, succeeded in the first half of the century in strengthening its constitutional position, but during the Wars of the Roses it became less truly representative of the solid part of the nation, the middle class, and more and more a party machine worked by the baronial factions. The proportion of people wanting peace and firm government steadily increased, and, when the internecine Wars of the Roses, which affected the lords and kings far more than the people, were followed by the protection and order provided without excessive cost by the Tudors, it was the people who most welcomed the change.

The towns were, however, comparatively little disturbed by these perpetual disorders. The mayors and corporations as a rule guided their cities through difficult times with politic shrewdness. Town life developed through flourishing trade and an increasing sense of municipal unity, and municipal importance.

Chapter 2

IMPORTANT FACTORS AFFECTING THE HISTORY OF YORK

Geographical Position

Among the factors affecting this particular city geographical position is evidently the most important. It is to this, combined with the consequent military value of the site, that York owes its origin as a city, its importance in the Middle Ages, and its practical importance today. York, which is the natural centre for the North of England, is the halfway house between London and Edinburgh, and is on the shortest and quickest land or air route, however the journey is made, between these two capitals. The Ouse and Humber have enabled it always to be within navigable distance of the North-East coast. The city itself is situated on an advantageous site in the centre of a great plain, the north and south ends of which are open. The surrounding hills and valleys are so disposed that a large number of rivers radiate towards the centre of the plain. Civilisation—if we must rank the ultra-fierce Norsemen, for instance, among its exponents—proceeded westwards from the coast, and wave after wave of the invading peoples crossed with ease the eastern and north-eastern hills, which are far less formidable than those on the west. York was already an important place in the days of Britain's making, the days when the land was in the melting-pot as far as race and nationality are concerned.

Important Factors Affecting the History of York

Military Value of Its Position

York is situated on the higher ground, in the angle made by the rivers Ouse and Foss at their junction; a little to the south, the east and the west there are low ridges of mound. The outer, main series of hills which border the central plain, are some dozen miles away, their outer faces being more or less parallel and running very roughly north and south. It seems clear that the site was chosen from the first for its immediate defensive value, the direct result of its geographical features. The position was of both tactical and strategic importance. In Roman times, however, its tactical value decreased when the great wall was built that stretched with its lines of mound, ditch, stone-rampart, and road, and its series of camps and forts, from near the mouth of the Tyne to Solway Firth. Henceforth the wall marked the debatable frontier, but York never lost its strategic value. It was thus used by the Romans, William I, Edward I, Edward II, and Edward III in their occupation of and their expeditions against the North. It has served as a base depot and military headquarters for centuries.

Political Importance

York, then, whatever its name (for it had many names) or condition, inevitably became an occupied place, a stronghold or a town from earliest times. When the Church attained great importance in the north, York, in addition to its natural and military values became, in 735, an ecclesiastical metropolis, for from this date the Archbishop of York was not only the ruler of the diocese of York, but in addition spiritual head of the Church in the North of England. Further, there were established in the city branches of the civil government. Business of the state, both civil and military, and of the Church was regularly conducted at York from early times. This political importance lasted long and is intimately connected with many events in the city's history. The fort and military defences were renewed from time to time, and staff-work and general administration, whether Roman or Edwardian, were conducted from York. The king, from whom York was rented by the citizens, had his official representatives with their offices permanently established here. The siege of 1644 after the royalist defeat at Marston Moor, was due mainly

Political Importance

to the political importance of the city. In Danish times there were kings of York. The Archbishops, besides owning large areas of land in and around the city, had their palace in the city. Monasteries grew up and flourished till the Dissolution; churches and other religious buildings were everywhere. Further, from century to century, York was the home of important nobles of the realm.

This political importance has persisted through the centuries. York still claims its traditional rank of second city in the kingdom.

Chapter 3

THE PLACES IN THE CITY

General Appearance

A general view of fifteenth-century York ("Everwyk" in Anglo-French and "Eboracum" in Latin) would give the impression of a very compact city within fortifications. Almost immediately it would be noticed how the three great elements of national society were very clearly reflected in the general appearance. First, the *Church,* the tremendous and ubiquitous power of which is emphasised by the strikingly beautiful and wonderfully constructed massive Minster, but so recently completed, standing, with its more than five hundred feet of length, its central tower two hundred feet high, most of its roofs a hundred feet or more above the ground, dwarfing the petty, storied dwellings. This is but one great church. In brilliant contrast in another quarter, adjoining the city, is the great abbey church of St. Mary, crowned by a lofty and magnificent spire rising above the equally fine conventual buildings. All over the city are seen the churches and buildings of other monastic and religious houses. The background of dwellings and shops, built in a similar style, is cut by a few winding streets, and studded with the towers, spires, and roofs of the multitude of parish churches. The intense and far-reaching influence of the Church in all phases of life is indelibly marked on this city.

The great influence of the royal *State,* second only to that of the Church, appears in the enclosing fortifications and especially in the solid stance of the Castle, where the keep stands out stoutly on its fortified mound. The whole castle, self-supporting within its own defences, its

General Appearance

massive walls, broad moats, outer and inner wards, protected gateways, drawbridges and other tactical devices, conveys an impression of power. On the Bishop-hill side of the river there remains the mound (Baile Hill) on which the other castle was erected by order of William the Conqueror. The whole city is enclosed by defensive works consisting of an embattled wall on a mound, with a moat or protecting ditch running parallel to it. At intervals along the walls there are towers. Where the four main roads enter the city there are the four gateways, or Bars, high enough to act as watch-towers and fit by their solid construction to offer a stout defence. The royal State keeps its stern watch around and within.

The third great element, the *People*, are represented by the few narrow, winding streets and the crowded houses, sending up blue smoke from their hearths, clustering round the great buildings of Church and State. The town itself is almost entirely in the eastern section of the city. On the western side the houses are grouped along the river bank and between Micklegate Bar and Ouse Bridge; there are several monasteries and churches in this section also. The third estate, the closely living masses, the people, has its outstanding buildings, but these are of comparatively local and small importance. Although the *city* and *guild* halls stand out utilitarian yet beautiful above the dwelling-houses, yet they are not at all so prominent as the great erections of the Church and the State.

A glance over the city today from the Walls or the top of a church tower emphasises the dominance of the cathedral over the whole city. The castle keep (Clifford's Tower) is still an important feature in the view. There were as rivals neither factories nor great commercial offices in the fifteenth-century city.

St. Clement's Nunnery and six churches, of which three were not far from Walmgate Bar and one was near Monk Bar, were actually outside the city walls.

Without the city and the cultivated land near by most of the country consisted of great stretches of forest,[1] i.e., wood, marsh, moor, wasteland. This surrounding forest-land was crossed by the few high-roads

---

1. Derived from Latin foris=outside, without (the city).

leading to and from the city, which they entered through the Bars. The country was not all wild and tenantless, for here and there, scattered about, were baronial castles and estates, and monastic houses and lands, all of which had their farming. In the forests there were villages each consisting of a few houses grouped together for common security, where lived minor officials and men working in the forest. The great Forest of Galtres, to the north of York, was a royal domain.

In the fifteenth century the population of York, the greatest city of the north, was about 14,000. Newcastle was the next greatest, being one of the ten or twelve leading cities of mediaeval England which had a total population of about 2–1/2 millions. The inhabitants of York registered in 1911 numbered 83,802.

Within the city there was a number of sub-entities, each self-contained and definitely marked off, often by enclosing, embattled walls. Such was the Minster, which stood within its close. The Liberty of the Minster of St. Peter included the parts of the city immediately round the Minster, the Archbishop's Palace, and the Bedern (a small district in the city where some of the Minster clergy lived collegiately), and groups of houses and odd dwellings scattered throughout other parts of the city and the county and elsewhere. Individual monasteries formed further such sub-entities; for instance St. Mary's Abbey, which was actually outside the city walls, but within its own defensive walls; the Franciscan Friary near the Castle; Holy Trinity Priory; the royal Hospital of St. Leonard. The Castle, which obviously had to be enclosed and capable of maintaining and enduring isolation, was independent of the city. Each of these ecclesiastical institutions enjoyed a large measure of freedom from the rule of the municipal authorities. The city was also subdivided into parishes, which, of course, were not enclosed by walls. The parish boundaries, although less well defined than those of the areas above mentioned, were none the less distinctly marked.

Streets

Streets, as we use the word today, were quite few in number. They were usually called gates and were mostly continuations of the great high-roads that came into and through the city, after crossing the wild country that covered most of northern England, a desert in which a city was an oasis and a sanctuary. In the lofty and graceful open lantern-tower of All Saints, Pavement, a lamp was hung to guide belated travellers to the safety and hospitality that obtained within the city walls. For the same purpose a bell was rung at St. Michael's, Ouse Bridge.

There were a few buildings along the high-roads just outside the great entrances, the Bars. Besides the few hovels and huts there were hospitals for travellers. There were four hospitals for lepers, the most wretched of all the sufferers from mediaeval lack of cleanliness.

Most of the streets were mere alleys, passages between houses and groups of buildings. They were very narrow and often the sky could hardly be seen from them because of the overhanging upper storeys of the buildings along each side. Goods in the Middle Ages and right down to the nineteenth century were carried in towns by hand. Carriages and waggons and carts were not very numerous and would have no need to proceed beyond the main streets and the open squares. If men must journey off their own feet, they rode horses. Pack-horses were used regularly to carry goods, where nowadays a horse or, more probably, a steam or motor engine would easily pull the goods conveniently placed on a cart or lorry.

The paving of rough cobbles and ample mud was distinctly poor. There was no adequate drainage; in fact there was very little attempt at any beyond the provision of gutters down the middle or at the sides of the streets. There were no regular street lights, and pavements, when they existed, were too meagre to be of much use to pedestrians.

Streets led to the two open market-places of this mediaeval city. Both of them (Thursday Market, now called St. Sampson's Square, and Pavement, which was a broad street with a market cross near one end) were used as markets, but for different kinds of produce. Some markets, such as the cattle market, were held in the streets. These two market-places were the principal public open spaces, parts of a town that are given such importance in modern town-planning schemes. Other open spaces were the cloisters and gardens of the monasteries, the courts of the Castle, the graveyards of the churches, and private gardens. In spite of these and the passage of a tidal river through the city, it cannot be denied that the inhabitants of our mediaeval city lived in rather dirty and badly ventilated surroundings.

The River Ouse was crossed by one bridge, which was of stone, with houses and shops of wood built up from the body of the bridge. The arches were small, and afford a striking contrast to the later constructions, in which a wide central arch replaced the two central small arches. The quays were just below the bridge. At one end of Ouse Bridge was St. William's Chapel, a beautiful little church,[1] as we know from the fragments of it that remain. Adjoining the chapel was the sheriffs' court; on the next storey was the Exchequer court; then there was the common prison called the Kidcote, while above these were other prisons which continued round the back of the chapel. Next to the prisons were the Council Chamber and Muniment Room. Opposite the chapel were the court-house, called the Tollbooth,[2] the Debtors' Prison, and a Maison Dieu, that is, a kind of almshouse.

The present streets called Shambles (formerly Mangergate),[3] Finkle Street, Jubbergate, Petergate, and especially Shambles, Little Shambles, and the passages leading from them, help one to realise the appearance of mediaeval streets and ways.

Buildings

Dwelling-houses ranged from big town residences of noble or distinguished families, by way of the beautifully decorated, costly houses of the rich middle-class merchants, to the humble dwellings of the poorest inhabitants. Every type of house from the palace to the hovel was well represented. The Archbishop's Palace, consisting of hall, chapel, quadrangle, mint, and gateway with prison, was near the Minster. Beyond the fine thirteenth-century chapel (now part of the Minster library buildings) hardly a trace of this undoubtedly splendid residence is left.

---

1. A "church" that was in a parish, but was not the parish church, was called a chapel. The parish church was the principal and parent church of all within the parish.
2. Compare the Tollbooth, Edinburgh, and the Tolhouse, Yarmouth.
3. Cf. French *manger*.

Buildings

The Percies had a great mansion in Walmgate. In other parts were the mansions of the Scropes and the Vavasours. It is, however, the houses of the prosperous traders that are the most interesting, for in them we see the kind of house a man built from the results of successful business. Most houses were of timber; those of the more wealthy were of stone and timber. The use of half-timbering, when the face of a building consisted of woodwork and plaster, made houses and streets very picturesque. The woodwork was often artistically carved. Each storey was made to overhang the one below it, so that an umbrella, if umbrellas had been in use then, would have been almost a superfluity, if not a needless luxury, besides being impossible to manipulate in the narrow streets and ways of a mediaeval city. The upper storeys of two houses facing each other across a street were often very close. Usually there were no more than three storeys. The roofs were very steep and covered generally with tiles, but in the case of the smaller dwellings with thatch. From a housetop the view across the neighbourhood would be of a huddled medley of red-tiled roofs, all broken up with gables and tiny dormer windows; there would be no regularity, just a jumble of patches of red-tiled roofing.

The present streets called Shambles, Pavement, Petergate and Stonegate, contain excellent examples of mediaeval domestic architecture.

Shops were distinguished by having the front of the ground floor arranged as a show-room, warehouse, or business room which was open to the street. The trader lived at his shop. In the case of a butcher's, for example, the front part of the shutters that covered the unglazed window at night, was let down in business hours so that it hung over the footway. On it were exhibited the joints of meat. Butchers' slaughter-houses were then, as now, private premises and right in the heart of the city.

The rooms in the houses were quite small, with low ceilings. The small windows, whether they were merely fitted with wooden shutters or glazed with many small panes kept together with strips of lead, lighted the rooms but poorly. The closeness of the houses made internal lighting still less effective. The interior walls were of timbering and plaster, often white- or colour-washed.[1] Panelling was used occasionally. The ventilation and hygienic conditions generally were far from good, as may be imagined from a consideration of the smallness of the houses, the compactness of the city, particularly the parts occupied by the people, and especially of the primitive system of sanitation, which was content to use the front street as a main sewer. There were, of course, no drains; at most there was a gutter along the middle of a street, or at each side of the roadway. It was the traditional practice to dump house and workshop refuse into the streets. Some of it was carried along by rainwater, but generally it remained: in any case it was noxious and dangerous. There was legislation on the subject, for the evil was already notorious in the fourteenth century. The first parliamentary attempt to restrain people in towns generally from thus corrupting and infecting the air is dated 1388. The many visits of distinguished people and public processions always conferred an incidental boon on the city, for one of the essentials of preparation was giving the main streets a good cleaning. There is no wonder that plagues perpetually harassed the people of mediaeval times and reduced the population miserably. The plague never disappeared till towns were largely rebuilt on a more commodious scale in the next great building era, which began in 1666 in London and in the early years of the eighteenth century elsewhere. No advance was made in sanitation till the Victorian Age, when town sanitation was completely revolutionised and, for the first time, efficiently organised.

The house fire was of wood and peat, though coal was also used. For artificial lighting oil-lamps (wicks in oil) and candles were used. A light was obtained from flint and tinder, the latter being ignited by a spark got from striking the flint with a piece of metal.

Rooms were furnished with chairs, tables, benches, chests, bedsteads, and, in some cases, tub-shaped baths. Carpets were to be found only in the houses of the very wealthy. The floors of ordinary houses, like those of churches, were covered with rushes and straw, among which it was the useful custom to scatter fragrant herbs. This rough carpet was pressed by the clogs of working people and the shoes of the fashionable. The spit was a much used cooking utensil. Table-cloths, knives, and spoons were in general use, but not the fork before the fifteenth

---

1. Wall-paper, which still bears the influence of the hangings that it replaced, came into general use early in the nineteenth century.

century. At one time food was manipulated by the fingers. York was advanced in table manners, for it is known that a fork was used in the house of a citizen family here in 1443. The richer members of the middle class owned a large number of silver tankards, goblets, mazer-bowls, salt-cellars and similar utensils and ornaments of silver, for this was a common form in which they held their wealth.

Beer, which was largely brewed at home, was the general beverage, but French and other wines were plentiful. The water supply came from wells, the water being drawn up by bucket and windlass, or from the river when the wells were low. The drinking water of the twentieth-century city is taken entirely from the River Ouse, but now the water is carefully treated and purified before reaching the consumer.

There were not many inns, as is shown in records by the number of innholders, who formed a trade company. There were also wine-dealers. Typical inn-signs were The Bull in Coney Street, and The Dragon. There is no reason to believe that in this century there was a really large amount of drinking and drunkenness, such as there was in the eighteenth century. An ordinance of the Marshals of 1409—"No man of the craft shall go to inns but if he is sent after, under pain of 4d."—may be quoted.

The houses of the wealthy and the great lords were, of course, the better furnished. They had walls adorned with tapestries and hung with arras or hangings; occasionally their walls were panelled. Their furniture was rich, well constructed, and carved by skilled craftsmen. Their mansions were large, for they had to house, beside the owner's family and personal household, retainers and dependents attached to his service in diverse capacities.

Civic Buildings consisted chiefly of the halls connected with the trade guilds. The rulers of the city and of the guilds were often the same men, in any case usually men of the same set. These secular buildings were really distinguished in appearance, but not monumental. They reflected something of the wealth that accrued from trade. They were of good size and proportions, built to be worthy of the practical use for which they were intended. The lower stages were of stone, the upper for the most part of wood and plaster (half-timbering). The structural framework was composed of stout beams and posts of timber. The timber roofs were covered with tiles. Examples may be seen in the Merchants' Hall, Fossgate, and St. Anthony's Hall in Peaseholm Green. The wooden roof of the Guild Hall, which was the Common Hall, erected in the fifteenth century, is supported by wooden columns. The walls of this hall and the entire basement are of stone.

Of Davy Hall, the King's administrative offices and prison for the Royal Forest of Galtres, not a trace remains to show the kind of buildings they were.

The Fortifications consisted of the Castle and the city Walls with their gateways. The massive stone Keep of the Castle was on a high artificial mound at the city end of the enclosed area occupied by the Castle. Around this mound there was a moat, or deep, broad ditch filled with water. The Keep, which is in plan like a quatrefoil, consisted of two storeys. Within, near the entrance, there is a well, the memory of which is for ever stained by the unhappy part it played in one of the most bitter persecutions of the Jews. Beyond the Keep there were inner and outer wards, official buildings including the King's great hall, the Royal Mint, and barracks for the King's soldiers. The entire Castle, which was the residence of the royal governor, and a military depot, was surrounded by walls, outside which were moats, or the river, or swamps, according to the position of each side. These moats, or defensive ditches, were crossed by drawbridges. To enter a fortified place in the Middle Ages one had to pass a barbican (i.e., an outwork consisting of a fortified wall along each side of the one way); a drawbridge across the moat; a portcullis or gate of stoutly inter-crossing timbers (set horizontally and vertically with only a small space between any two beams, giving the whole gate the appearance of a large number of small square holes, each surrounded by solid wood) that could be lowered or raised at will in grooves at the sides of the entrance opening. The ends of the vertical posts at the bottom formed a row of spikes which were shod with iron. The points of these spikes entered the ground when the portcullis was lowered. Beyond, there were the wooden gates of the inner opening.

The city Walls, of which the present remains date from the reign of Edward III, were broad, crenellated walls of limestone, on a high mound which was protected without by a parallel deep moat. At the north, east, south, and west corners there were massive bastions, and be-

Buildings

tween these, at short intervals, smaller towers. Besides being crenellated the raised front of the wall itself was often pierced with slits shaped for the use of long or cross-bows. The bowmen were very well protected by these skilful arrangements. Some of these slits, shaped like crosses, were of exquisite design architecturally.

The continuity of these mural fortifications was broken only where swamps and the rivers made them unnecessary and where roads passed through them. The four principal entrances along the main high-roads were defended by the four Bars, or fortified gateways. These, with their Barbicans, three of which were so needlessly and callously destroyed in the last century, were magnificent examples of noble permanent military architecture. The outer facade of Monk Bar today, spoiled as it is, expresses a noble strength. There was formerly only the single way, both for ingress and egress.[1] The Bar was supported on each side by the mound and wall, which latter led right into the Bar and so to the corresponding wall on the other side. Each of these entrances to the city was protected by barbican, portcullis, and gate. Each evening the Bars were closed and the city shut in for the night. Defenders used a Bar as a watch-tower or a fort. They could walk along the high crenellated walls of the Barbican and shoot thence, and stop the way by lowering the portcullis.[2]

Near the Castle there were the Castle mills, where the machinery was driven by water-power.

Outside the walls there were strays, or common lands. Some of the land immediately around the city was cultivated or used as pasture. There were, besides dwellings, several churches and hospitals, just outside the city. Beyond this suburban area was the forest.

The most notable of the *Religious Buildings* is the Minster, which was practically completed in the fifteenth century, when the work of erecting

---

1. The view today from Petergate towards Bootham Bar gives a good impression of a narrow main street, with gabled houses, leading to the single fortified opening provided by the Bar.

2. The winch and portcullis are still in existence in Monk Bar, and in working order.

the three towers was finished. The architectural splendour of this mighty church must have appealed very strongly to the people of the fifteenth century, for did they not see the great work that had gone on for centuries at last brought to this glorious conclusion? It rose up in the midst of the city, always visible from near and far. The inside was even more magnificent than the exterior. The fittings and furniture were of the richest. The light mellow tone of the white stonework was enhanced by the fleeting visions of colour that spread across from the sunlit stained-glass windows, which still, in spite of time and restoration, add enormously to the beauty of the interior.

The Minster stood within its Close, one of the four gateways of which, College Street Arch, remains. This part of the city around the Minster was enclosed because it was under the jurisdiction of the Liberty of St. Peter.

Originally founded in 627 by Edwin, King of Northumbria, the Minster had been rebuilt and enlarged from time to time. It received its final and present form in the fifteenth century. At one time the Nave was rebuilt: at the same time there was built, near but separate from the main building, the Chapter House, a magnificent octagonal parliament house of one immense chamber: later the Chapter House was connected with the main building by the Vestibule. Then the Choir was replaced by a larger and finer building in the then latest architectural fashion. The new choir contained the east window, which in the eyes of contemporaries was wonderful and unrivalled for its size and painted glass. It occupies nearly all the central space of the east wall from a few feet above the ground to almost the apex of the gable. Gothic architecture was so marvellously adaptable that all these parts, built at widely different times, at various and strongly-contrasted stages of the development of this English mediaeval architecture, together make a single building that appears to possess the most felicitous unity of general design and a perfectly wonderful diversity of sectional design, for every part is in complete sympathy with the scheme as a whole.

To the east of the Central Tower is the Choir, which was kept exclusively for the services; to the west, the Nave, the popular part. The entrance to the Choir from the west is made through the stone screen of Kings, which, with the lofty organ which rests on it, prevents people in the Nave from getting anything more than a glimpse of what is taking place in the Choir. Over the western ends of the Nave aisles are the twin west towers, which contain the bells. The high altar and reredos stood in the middle of the Choir between the two choir transepts, the huge windows of which present in picture the life stories of St. Cuthbert and St. William respectively. The Lady Chapel, the part of the choir to the east of the reredos, was very important in pre-Reformation days when the cult of the Virgin was very popular. To the north and south of the Central Tower are the Transepts. From the North Transept the Vestibule leads to the Chapter House. The church is, therefore, of the shape of a cross (the centre of which is marked by the Central Tower) with an octagonal building standing near and connected with the northern arm.

The furniture was of wood and elaborately carved. In the Choir were the fixed stalls with towering canopies, and other seats, which were ranged along the north and south sides and at the west end. Chapels were marked off by wooden screens, often of elaborate tracery.

The cost of erecting this huge and splendid church must have been enormous. The Minster contained the shrine of St. William of York, which, like those of St. Cuthbert at Durham and St. Thomas at Canterbury of European fame, attracted streams of pilgrims, whose donations helped the funds of erection and maintenance. This was an established means of raising funds for church purposes. There was, also, the money from penances and indulgences. The Archbishops were keenly interested in their cathedral church. Citizens gave and bequeathed sums of money to the Minster funds. In addition, the Minster authorities received gifts from wealthy nobles of the north of England. The house of Vavasour, for instance, supplied stone; that of Percy gave wood to be used in building the great metropolitan church. If the money cost was enormous, the completed building, for design, engineering, and decorative work—in stone, wood, cloth, stained glass—was far beyond monetary value.

The Nave, the part open to the public, was used for processions; some started from the great west door, entrance through which was a rare privilege granted only to the highest. The Choir was the scene of the daily services of the seven offices of the day. All around, in the aisles and transepts, were altars in side-chapels, chantry-chapels,[1] where throughout the early part of the day priests were saying masses for the souls of the departed. There were thirty chantries in the Minster.

The Minster has from its foundation been a cathedral. The Chapter of canons with the Dean at their head has always been its Governing Body. As a church it was served by prebendaries or canons, who had definite periods of duty annually, and two residential bodies of priests, of whom some, the chantry priests, lived at St. William's College. This College was erected shortly after the middle of the fifteenth century: on the site there had been Salton House, the prebendal residence of the Prior of Hexham, who was canon of Salton. This picturesque building of stone, wood, half-timber work, and tiled roofs is a little to the east of the Minster. It consists of a series of rooms ranged round a central courtyard. It is of much historical interest, and since it was restored recently to be the home of the Convocation of the Northern Province, it has returned to the service of the church. The minor-canons, or vicars-choral, who were employed by the canons as their deputies, also lived in community. They had their hall, chapel, and other buildings in an enclosed part called the Bedern not far from the Minster.

As a counterpart to the Minster, in appearance as in use, was the great, rich Benedictine Abbey of St. Mary, of royal foundation. With a mitred abbot who sat among the lords spiritual in Parliament, St. Mary's was perhaps the most important of the northern monasteries. The buildings were proportionally large and fine. The church, dating mostly from the thirteenth and fourteenth centuries, was particularly long and had a tall spire. It was only a little inferior to the Minster in magnificence. On the south side were the Cloisters, the open-air work-place and recreation place of the monks, while beyond were the conventual buildings—such as the calefactory or warming-house, the dormitories,

---

1. The Leschman Chantry Chapel in Hexham Abbey is a typical example in excellent preservation. A small erection of stone and wood, it stands between two of the piers of the north Choir arcade. In small compass there are a stone altar with five crosses, an aumbry beneath the altar, and the tomb with recumbent effigy of the founder. A priest would have just sufficient room to move about in the performance of his service. Part of Archbishop Bowet's tomb in York Minster was a chantry chapel.

and the refectory or room where meals were taken. The cloisters were square in plan and consisted of a central grass plot, along the sides of which there was a continuous covered walk with unglazed windows facing the central open space. Benedictine abbeys usually conformed to a common scheme as regards the planning of the church and the conventual buildings. The cloisters were only one of the courts or open squares, which separated groups of conventual buildings. Further, there were gardens and orchards. Nearer the river there was the Hospitium, or guesthouse, where visitors were lodged. The abbey was within its own walls, and on one side its grounds extended to the river. The gateway, comprising gate, lodge, and chapel, was on the north side.

Near the Castle there was an extensive Franciscan Friary. On the other side of the river there was the priory of the Holy Trinity, the home of an alien Benedictine order. A Carmelite Friary in Hungate, opposite the Castle, seems, from the few odd fragments of stone that remain, to have had fine buildings. The Augustinian Friary was between Lendal and the river. The Dominican house, which was burnt down in 1455, was on the site of the old railway station.

The only nunnery in the city was the Benedictine Priory of St. Clement. There were sisterhoods in St. Leonard's and other hospitals. It should, however, be noted there were many nunneries in the districts round York.

Some of the religious institutions were called Hospitals. The care of the sick was only one of the functions of this type of religious house. Such was the large and famous St. Leonard's Hospital, a royal institution that was not under the control of a bishop. The beautiful ruins of St. Leonard's, which adjoined St. Mary's Abbey, prove how well this hospital had been built. These hospitals, of which there were fifteen in York, were in close touch with the people. While St. Mary's, for instance, was one of the great abbeys, where the monks, by the time when the fifteenth century was advanced, were living luxuriously, easily, and generally unproductively, the religious of the hospitals and lesser houses, were still engaged in feeding the poor, tending the sick, and educating the children of the people.

Each of these religious institutions, whether monastery or hospital, was within its own grounds, bounded by its own walls. Altogether they occupied a large part of the total area of the mediaeval city which their buildings adorned, and of which they were so characteristic a feature: St. Mary's Abbey, which with its buildings and grounds covered a large area, was actually outside the city proper, but it was immediately adjoining it. There were nearly sixty monasteries, priories, hospitals, maisons-dieu, and chapels. The maisons-dieu, of which there were sixteen, were smaller hospitals. They combined generally the duties of almshouse and chantry.

Parish Churches, which were the centres of the religious life of the laity, were everywhere. In the fifteenth century there were forty-five churches and ten chapels, so that there was always a place in church for every citizen.

A church was always in use. Besides the regular public services which took place frequently during the day, and the special services for festivals, there were services in chantries. Both the high altar in the chancel and altars in other parts of a church were used. Several altars were necessary because the number of masses, for the celebration of which money was liberally bequeathed, was very large. The parish church was used for other than purely religious purposes. It was the central meeting-place of the parish, and might be described as the seat of parochial government. Meetings were held in the Nave. Parts of the church were used as schools. The parish church was also the depot for the equipment of those members who became soldiers. Moreover, fire-buckets (generally of leather) were often kept in the church, since, being of stone, it was perhaps the safest building in the parish. There were also long poles with hooks at the end used to pull thatch away from burning houses.

Most, if not all, of these churches were fine specimens of the architecture of the Middle Ages, the so-called Gothic architecture, which is characterised by pointed arches, ribbed vaulting, and the constant use of the buttress. These churches were, in contrast to the present condition of most of those that remain, complete with chancel, nave and aisles, towers or spires, bells, stained-glass windows, and furniture, many of them being particularly rich in one or more of these features. The painted windows[1] are especially interesting, for they show the standard of this branch of fifteenth-century art and are valuable historical documents. The rich, mellow tones of colour should be noted, also the inci-

Buildings

dental pictures of mediaeval dress and furniture. It is interesting to compare the fifteenth-century work with that done, for instance, by the William Morris firm to the designs of Burne-Jones (1833–1898), at a time when the revived art, with other forms of decoration, was enjoying a period of great success. In the fifteenth century the church was flourishing materially, at least, and money and gifts were freely given.

The offices and services in churches were recited and sung. Organs were used, but were not very large and were capable of being carried about: although working on similar principles to the modern organ they lacked its size, power, and varied capacity. At the Minster there were several organs, for instance "the great organs," "the organs in the Choir," "the organs at the Altar B.V.M."

The Chancel was the most sacred part of the church, for there was the principal or high altar. In the Chancel were the stalls or seats of the clergy and officials. The actual seats could be turned up when the occupants wished to stand. Standing for long periods was made less irksome in that the underside of each seat was made with a projecting ledge, which gave some support. It is thoroughly characteristic of the age that this very human device should have existed, and, secondly, that these ledges were carved and ornamented. These misericords, as they are called, were usually curiously, even grotesquely carved. Some of these carvings were founded on natural objects, some were grotesque heads, others represented subjects with man and animals. There were pews for the nobility, but, apart from the few old and weak people who used the rough bench or two in the body of the church, or the stone bench that ran along the walls, the general public stood during the services.

Wealthy parishioners left money to the parochial clergy and for the fabric of the church: they generally wished to be buried at some particular place within their parish church. Such distinguished men as Nicholas Blackburn, merchant of York, were commemorated at times in their parish churches by means of stained-glass windows. The portraits of

---

1. Besides the exceptional display of fifteenth-century glass in the Minster, notable examples occur in St. Martin's, Coney Street, All Saints,' North Street, and Holy Trinity, Goodramgate.

Nicholas and his son and their wives appear in the east window of All Saints,' North Street; his arms also are to be seen in this window.

York As a Port

The Ouse was tidal and navigable right up to York. Trade, especially in woollen goods, was carried on in the fifteenth century by river and sea directly between York and ports on the west coasts of the continent and, especially, Baltic ports. On arriving at York the boats stopped at the quays, adjacent to which were warehouses, just below Ouse Bridge.

The sea-going boats were not large. They were usually one-masted sailing ships, built of wood; they had high prows and sterns, with a capacious hold between. Some of them were built in York.

Their trade was such that some of the York merchants, for example the wealthy Howme family, had establishments in foreign ports. The Howmes had property in Calais.

The regulation of the waterways in and near the city was vested in the Corporation. Matters pertaining to navigation and shipping were adjudged by an Admiralty Court under the King's Admiral, whose jurisdiction extended from the Thames to the northern ports.

Chapter 4

Everyday Life in the City

Civic Life

"Parish government formed the unit in the government of the city. Each parish was a self-governing community, electing its own officers with the exception of its rector, making its own bye-laws, and, to meet expenses, levying and collecting its own rates. Its constables served as policemen, attended the Sessions, and acted as the fire brigade. They looked after the parish-trained soldiers, acted as recruiters, and had the care of the parish armour, which was kept in a chest in the church. They distributed money among lame soldiers, gathered trophy money, relieved cripples and passengers, but unfeelingly conveyed beggars and vagabonds to prison. The parish soldiers kept watch and ward over the parish defences. The parish stocks, in which offenders were placed, stood near the churchyard stile. The constables were also responsible for such lighting as the parish required, and kept the parish lanthorn.

"The officials looked after the parish poor, dispensing charity by gifts of bread and money. The parish boundaries were perambulated every Ascension Day. Parish dinners were held on the choosing of the churchwardens, the visitation of the Archdeacon, etc. The parish officials invoked the aid of the law when parochial rights were infringed, especially by neighbours. The church was the centre of parochial life and in it the business of the parish was transacted.

"Parishes were grouped as wards. The wards chose city Councillors, and these elected their Aldermen. The six wards formed the municipality over which presided the Mayor. The Corporation exercised a general supervision over the whole of the parishes of which there were forty-five.

"Gradually the duties and powers of the various parish officials have been transferred to the City Council. The united parish soldiers became the city trained bands. In 1900 the last remnant of parochial officialdom passed into the power of the Corporation when parish overseers ceased to exist, and, for rating purposes, the City of York became one parish instead of the original forty-five separately rated areas."[1]

The Cathedral, i.e., the Liberty of St. Peter, and the Royal Castle were outside municipal control. The Archbishops also had their privileges. They had once owned all the city on the right bank of the Ouse. In the fifteenth century they still retained many of their privileges and possessions in this quarter, as, for example, the right of holding a fair here in what was formerly their shire. These archiepiscopal rights have not all lapsed, for in 1807 the Archbishop of the time, successfully asserting his legal rights, saved from demolition the city walls on the west side of the river.

York was a royal borough, that is, the freemen of the city had to pay rent to the king, from whom it was farmed directly. It was not owned by any knight or lord, that is, apart from the Archbishop's possessions, which belonged to the western section of the city; the city proper was almost entirely on the opposite side of the river. The King retained possession of certain properties, such as Galtres Forest, lying in the valley stretching northwards from York. He had a larder and a fish pond at York; also a court, offices, and a prison (Davy Hall, of which the name alone remains) for the administration of the forest. These town-properties were, of course, entirely extra-parochial.

York received a long succession of royal charters. Henry I granted the city certain customs, laws and liberties, and the right to have a merchant guild. The possession of these rights was confirmed by King John in the first year of his reign. In 1396 Richard II, at York, made the city a county in itself. In consequence the office of bailiff was replaced by that of sheriff.

---

1. G. Benson: "Parish of Holy Trinity, Goodramgate, York."

Civic Life

The King's official representative in the city was called the sheriff, whose office in York has been continuous down to the present day. The sheriffs—there were usually two—were responsible for the maintenance of order, for the local soldiery, and the collection of the royal taxes and dues. The sheriff was a busy and important mediaeval official.

The Mayor was the real governor of the city. He was a powerful official and literally ruler of the city. In practice he was most often a wealthy and important merchant; and, like the Aldermen, belonged to the group of men who governed the trade guilds as well as the municipality. Various symbols were attached to his office. The chief objects among the corporation regalia at the present time are the sword, mace, and cap of maintenance.

There were three city councils, "the twelve," "the twenty-four," and "the forty-eight," as they were called. There were the Aldermen and Councillors—the "lords" and "commons" of the municipal parliament. The ordinary council-chamber was at Ouse Bridge: the other was the Common Hall, the present Guildhall. Sometimes the whole community of citizens met, when for the moment the government of the city became essentially and practically democratic. This was only done on important occasions to decide broad questions of policy, or when numbers were needed to enforce a decision. The commons really possessed no administrative power. The form of civic government was supposed to be representative, but as a matter of fact it was not only not founded on popular election (a procedure enforced in 1835 by the Municipal Reform Act), but was kept exclusively in the hands of the wealthy merchant and trading class, the middle class. Men of this class became Aldermen. When a vacancy occurred in the upper house of civic government, they chose a man like themselves. The Mayor was elected by the Aldermen, who naturally chose one of themselves. In fact the government of the city was in the hold of a "close self-elected Corporation."

The civic spirit developed a good deal during the fifteenth century, no doubt in connection with the simultaneous increase in the wealth and social pretension of the rising merchant middle class. It appeared in the greater respect bestowed on the office of Mayor and the pomp and reverence attached to his position. The "right worshipful" the Mayor and the Aldermen wore rich state robes edged with fur. In addition, contemporary city records reflect the new spirit in such expressions as "the worshupful cite," "the said full honourabill cite," "this full nobill city." This spirit, however, developed more fully in the sixteenth century.

The Mayor held his court in the Common Hall, where he heard pleas about apprentices and mysteries (i.e., the rules of the crafts); offences against the customs of the city; breaches of the King's peace. It was his duty to administer the statute merchant. The Recorder was the official civic lawyer.

The governors of the city were intimately connected with the control of trade, and the rule of the pageants. These phases of city life overlapped considerably and were interdependent. Weaving was the principal trade. The Mayor and Aldermen were the masters of the mysteries of the weavers. Power to enforce the ordinances of the other mysteries was granted by the Mayor and Corporation.

There were times when the King took the government into his own hands. This was done during the rebellion of the Percies, a northern family skilled and experienced in rebelling. Henry IV withdrew the right of government from the city in 1405, but he restored it in 1406 after the execution of Archbishop Scrope, who had been so popular with the people of York.

Of mediaeval punishments the most obvious were the stocks, a contemporary picture of which is to be seen in one of the stained-glass windows of All Saints,' North Street. Examples of stocks survive in the churchyards of Holy Trinity, Micklegate, and St. Lawrence's. They were near the entrance to the churchyard and commanded full public attention. The petty offender, condemned to spend so many hours in the public gaze and subject to whatever treatment the public chose to inflict on him, sat on the ground or on a low seat, while his feet were secured at the ankles by two vertical boards. The upper was raised for the insertion of the ankles in the specially cut-out half-round holes in each board, so that when the boards were touching and in the same vertical plane, the ankles were completely surrounded by wood.

To its political importance York owed the ghastly exhibition of heads and odd quarters of traitors and others who had gained punishment of national importance, which usually consisted of "hanging, drawing and quartering," when the quarters and the head were sent to London and the principal towns of the kingdom to be exhibited on gateways, towers, and bridges. This practice served to provide the public with convincing proof that a traitor was actually dead, and was very necessary in an age when Rumour, "stuffing the ears of men with false reports" held sway over "the blunt monster with uncounted heads, the still discordant wavering multitude." Micklegate Bar was so used. In Shakespeare's *Henry VI* Queen Margaret makes, with reference to the Duke of York, this bitter play of words:—

"Off with his head and set it on York gates;
So York may overlook the town of York."

One very interesting practice in connection with the mediaeval system of law and policing was the use of the right of sanctuary. The monasteries, the Minster, and all churches had this right of giving a sacrosanct safety to criminals and others flying from their pursuers, whether officers of the law or the general mob, whose right, be it noted, it was to join in the chase after offenders (the "hue and cry") and help to arrest them. Provided the pursued reached the prescribed area, which, in some cases, as at the nationally famous sanctuary of St. John of Beverley, prevailed for some distance from the church itself, he was safe from his pursuers. Hexham Abbey and Beverley Minster still exhibit their sanctuary chairs or frith-stools. In the north door of Durham Cathedral there is an ancient, massive knocker, the rapper, of the form of a ring, being held in the mouth of a grotesque head. The frith-stool, to which the seeker went at once, stood near the high altar at which he made his declarations on oath. His case was carefully investigated and often sanctuary-seekers were allowed to exile themselves from the kingdom. The coroner was the public officer of inquiry. The Church took every care that the crime of breaking the sanctuary so granted was regarded not at all lightly. The right of sanctuary, after being changed to apply to certain towns only—among them York—continued till it was ended by law in the reign of James I

Condemned heretics were burnt[1] at Tyburn, the site of local executions, some way from Micklegate Bar along the main south road.

Everyday Life in the City

Parliamentary and National Life

According to the general principle, the King was the ultimate and absolute owner and ruler of the land and people. The rights, liberties, customs, and powers possessed by individuals and corporate bodies were specified parts of the royal power which the King had granted on some consideration or other. Thus, knights, archbishops, and nobles received lands and rights in return for the provision, when required, of military service by themselves and a certain force of their retainers, except that no personal military service was required from the archbishop from the very nature of his calling. The monasteries and other Church institutions had many possessions and rights. The Church, which was established in the realm before Parliament, was a very great owner of land. The authorities of cities, with their trade-guilds, received the right of trading, or holding markets, and of levying tolls or municipal taxes. They received also the right of making their own local laws or bye-laws. These authorities, whether individuals or corporate bodies, to whom rights and liberties were granted, had their own officers and laws controlling their liberties. Besides the King's peace, there were, therefore, the jurisdictions of these various rights granted from the supreme royal authority.

From York there went to the national Parliament the lord Archbishop of York, the lord Abbot of St. Mary's Abbey, those nobles who resided in the city and were Lords Temporal, and the two representatives of the commonalty of the city. The body of Lords Spiritual was of great importance in the Middle Ages. The Convocation of the lords of the Church had itself a share in the governing of the nation as well as of the Church, its own particular sphere. The Church was one of the most powerful and richest factors in national affairs. The clear division of the Parliament of the Middle Ages into three groups reflects the sharp divisions

---

1. *De heretico comburendo,* 1401. In 1539 Valentine Freez, a freeman, and his wife, were burnt at the stake on Knavesmire for heresy. Frederick Freez, Valentine's father, was a book-printer and a freeman (1497).

that there were between the three great classes of the nation—the nobles, the clergy, the people.

In the fifteenth century, as in other centuries, York was frequently visited by the King. From time to time, as when the King and Court proceeded north during the wars with Scotland, Parliament was moved to York, where it was held in the Chapter House of the Minster. Six of the seven windows of the Chapter House contain their original stained glass, in which appear shields of King Edward I and members of the Court. The Chapter House was used as a Parliament house during the reigns of the first three Edwards. The King, in mediaeval times, was actual commander-in-chief, and it suited him well for Parliament to meet in the political capital of the north, so that he could continue the civil administration while conducting warfare in the north.

Henry IV was in York on several occasions, chiefly because of rebellions. The house of Percy, which engaged frequently in revolt and faction, led the rebellion of 1403 in which Henry Percy, called Hotspur, was killed at the battle of Shrewsbury. Harry Hotspur, whom Shakespeare made in accordance with tradition the fiery and valorous counterpart of Prince Hal, Henry IV's heir and Falstaff's companion, was buried in the Minster. When Archbishop Scrope headed a revolt, also not unconnected with the Percies, from York and was arrested, Henry IV hastened to York, and the popular archbishop was executed forthwith, a royal and sacrilegious deed that caused intense indignation especially among the people of York, who for some months lost the right of local government as a result of this affair.

The Wars of the Roses (1455–1485), a long internecine feud between kings, lords, and landed gentry, affected the towns but little. The baronage suffered heavily, the middle class lightly. No town ever stood a siege, while Towton was the only battle in which the common soldiers had heavy losses. Warwick made it a practice to spare the commoners, whereby he conciliated the people. Under Yorkist rule, after the decisive battle of Towton (1461) England can be described as not unprosperous. One very notable feature was the immense amount of building that was done, and that not so much of castles, as of country houses, churches, and cathedrals, so many of which splendidly adorn the land today. The only people seriously affected by the Wars of the Roses were the main participants. Compared with modern warfare, which is unabated scientific extermination, mediaeval warfare was often of the nature of a mild adventure. The size of the opposing forces was very small even compared with the scanty population. The chief weapons were lances, swords, long-bows, and cross-bows, but protective armour was worn. The fighting was generally sporadic and desultory and the casualties were very few.

It was at York that Henry VI awaited the news of the result of the battle of Towton. Edward IV entered York as victor after the battle. York, like other cities at the time, took care to maintain the good graces of both sets of combatants. Although through the Wars of the Roses national parliamentary government ultimately broke down and gave way to the strong personal kingship of Henry VII, the towns, which actually suffered little, increased their local powers. Civic government developed much and trade flourished during the century.

York had a good friend in Richard, Duke of Gloucester. The city was very loyal to him and helped him by raising troops in his support. When he visited York he was received with immense festivity and magnificence. The Mayor and Corporation in their correspondence with him addressed him as "our full tender and especial good lord." They had to thank him "for his great labour now late made unto ye king's good grace for the confirmation of the liberties of this city." But for his death at Bosworth, York would have benefited greatly by his munificence.

Henry VII was in York in 1487. After Bosworth (1485) the city had assured him of its loyalty. The marriage of Henry of Richmond, who represented the House of Lancaster, and Elizabeth, daughter of Edward IV Duke of York, fittingly followed the conclusion of the Wars of the Roses. With Henry VII's reign a new era began in English history.

Throughout the century the city could not avoid contact with rival parties and powers. In spite, however, of rebellions and the Wars of the Roses, the capital of the north managed generally to steer a safe course through many storms.

Other links with national affairs were the periodic visits of the King's judges who travelled on circuit over the country, stopping at important centres to hold assize there. Their duties consisted not only in settling matters of litigation, but also in reviewing the way in which all the

King's affairs were being conducted in each locality. They supervised the work of the sheriffs.

Galtres Forest and the Fish Pond, both royal property, helped to furnish the king's table with food. From the royal Larder at York such foodstuffs as venison, game, and fish were despatched salted to wherever the King required them.

Business Life

Business, in one form or another, was the occupation of the majority of the citizens. There were a few capitalist merchants, many traders, and thousands of employed workpeople, skilled and unskilled. Such street names as Spurriergate, Fishergate, Girdlergate, Hosier Lane, and Colliergate would suggest that men in the same trade had their premises in the same quarter, possibly in the same street.

The English middle class, which had taken form in the fourteenth century, was well established in the fifteenth century, when it became so important as to be an appreciable factor in the national life. The middle class arose through currency, the use of money to bring in more money by trading. Trade became the monopoly of the middle class, the successful master-traders. It was men of this class, the capitalist employers, the merchants and traders who were the mayors and aldermen, who ruled the city. The exclusiveness, which was eminently characteristic of this class, appeared especially in their attitude towards national taxation and in that towards trade organisations. With regard to taxation the towns persistently avoided the assessment of individual traders, who did not wish to disclose the amount of their wealth, by agreeing that the whole town should pay to the Exchequer a sum to be raised by the Mayor and Corporation. The middle class achieved its aims politically by transformation from within. Instead of making a direct assertive attack, these master-traders usually so developed their own interests within the established institutions (such as the guilds) that they ultimately gained their object quietly and shrewdly. This class established itself against the King and the nobles on the one hand, and during the century in effective fashion against the workers on the other. This appears in the more definite distinctions of class among the citizens that arose. The masters had got the control of the guilds into their own power. While maintaining the original outward appearance of the guilds as societies of men affected by the same interests in daily life, the employers had actually become a powerful vested class that ruled both city and guild life. In the fifteenth century the workmen were founding fraternities of their own.

Memory of the Jews, the money-dealers of other times, survived if only from the harrowing stories of the various persecutions that had taken place all over England, and not least in York. The Jews had been expelled from the country by Edward I, with the encouragement of the Church, in 1290, partly for economic, partly for religious reasons. Their supplanters, the Italian bankers, whom Edward favoured, soon acquired from their trading an unpopularity equal to that of the Jews as traders. The rise of the middle class had coincided with the release of money in coin from the hoards of the Jews, and from the coffers of the Knights Templars, whose order was abolished in 1312.

The merchant and trading class, apart from the nobility and the Church, formed the bulk of the people of the nation. They were the solid part of the nation, that paid taxes, that supplied clerks, monks, and priests, that liberally supported the Church, that kept the nation progressive and solvent by commercial undertakings.

The professions, as we use the term today, had not as yet attained sufficient importance for them to form a distinct class division. There were a few capable physicians, but generally the practice of medicine was shared by the Church and the barber-surgeons. Priests and officers of the Church had the privilege peculiar to the Church by which even a poor but intellectually capable man could rise to high office and become the social equal of nobles. Architecture was practised by master-masons under the patronage of leading ecclesiastics and nobles. Teaching was nearly all the work of the Church. The lawyers, however, were already to be distinguished from those who gained profit by dealing in goods, for they made profit from transactions on paper, from managing the interests of others, from trading in their own acute mental powers.

The wool trade was by far the most extensive and flourishing trade of England in the fourteenth and fifteenth centuries. This was the trade that made England great commercially. Wool was England's raw material and the source of most of her wealth. The numerous monasteries had huge sheep-farms. Edward III had encouraged foreign clothworkers to settle in England (in York, as in other places). The first York craftsmen to be incorporated were the weavers, who received a charter from Henry II, in return for which they paid a tax to the King for the customs and liberties he granted them. The weavers were the largest and wealthiest body of traders.

Guilds had developed from societies of masters and men engaged in the same trade, to the trade-guilds, which in the fourteenth century were trade corporations, the lower ranks of members being the workers, the higher ranks, including the office-holders, the richer merchants, the capitalist employers. The ruling committees of the trade-guilds made regulations and generally governed their particular trades. Despite the power of the guilds the municipal authority maintained its supremacy in civic government because it enforced the ordinances of the trades. Moreover, disputes between the guilds themselves gave the city authority opportunities of increasing its power, of which it availed itself.

The system of serfdom, by which serfs were bound to a particular domain and owned by their overlord, had not yet ceased. Nearly all the workmen of York, however, were freemen, i.e., they had full and complete citizenship. The members of the councils of aldermen and councillors, the mayors and city officials, the members of the trade-guilds, were all freemen.

In the fifteenth century the wealthy and important employers and traders governed the guilds. They were in the position and had the power to regulate the conduct in every way of their own trades. Thus, rules were laid down as to the terms of admission of men to the practice of a trade; the government of the guild and the meetings of the members and ruling committees; the moral standard of the members in their work and trafficking; the payments of masters to workers; the prices of goods to be sold to the public or other traders; the rates of fines and the amount of confiscations inflicted on those who broke the rules of their guild; the terms on which strangers, English and foreign, were to be allowed to pursue their trade in the city; whether Sunday trading was to be permitted or not; the duties of the searchers; everything incident to the share of the guild in the city's production of pageant plays.

Everyday Life in the City

The question of the terms of the residence and trading of strangers received constant consideration. The city had, in many respects, complete local autonomy and rules were made with regard to strangers who came to carry on their trades in the city. From 1459 aliens had, by municipal law, to live in one place only, at the sign of the Bull in Coney Street, unless they received special permission from the Mayor to reside elsewhere. The guilds were ruled by masters and wardens. They had their various officials. The searchers were officers appointed to observe that the rules of the trade were being carried out properly. They took care that only authorised members pursued the trade of the guild of which they were the officers. They vigilantly watched the conduct of the members, and it was their duty to take action in case of infringement of the rules and to bring offenders before the Mayor in his court.

The wealthy trading class all over the country did great and lasting work in founding grammar schools and building or rebuilding cathedrals and churches or parts of them. There was a social side to the guilds. This appeared in the public processions and the performances of plays, the morality and mystery plays of mediaeval England. There was also a strong religious side to the guilds. The processions and plays were fundamentally religious. The Church's festivals were recognised as holidays. Much money was given and bequeathed for the foundation of chantries, which with their priests have their place also in the educational life of the city.

The merchants lived well. They were rich from trade, and through the corporate guilds governed their own trades both legislatively and executively; the highest offices in civic life were theirs; they lived in houses as splendid as they cared to have them; they furnished their homes with quantities of silver plate, both for use and for ornament, for this was the most suitable outlet for superfluous wealth in days when modern facilities for investment did not exist; they wore clothes of fine material, richly trimmed; they were honoured citizens; they were earnest in religion and their benevolence to the Church is very remarkable. They were forming a lesser aristocracy now that they were becoming owners of agricultural land as well as town property. They had the benefits of wealth and comfort, while they were shrewd enough to avoid the penalties of advertised riches. A typical instance of a successful merchant who rose to

Business Life

high positions was that of Sir Richard Yorke, who was Mayor of the staple of Calais and Lord Mayor of York in 1469 and 1482, and member of Parliament. A window in St. John's Church, Micklegate, in commemoration of him is still to be seen. A shield bearing his arms (azure, saltire argent) appears in the glass; another bears the arms of the Merchants of the Wool staple of Calais. He was knighted by Henry VII when that king was in York in 1487.

Masters took apprentices, who themselves generally became masters in their turn. The conditions of apprenticeship were ruled in detail by the guilds.

When a workman became a skilled artisan he was called a journeyman,[1] that is, a man who earned a full day's pay for his work. The legal hours of work were, from March to September, from 5 A.M. to 7.30 P.M., with half an hour for breakfast, and an hour and a half for dinner. Saturday was universally a half-holiday. There were 44 working weeks in a year and, consequently, a total of holidays and non-working times of eight weeks. The burden of the very long hours was increased by the great physical exertion required from men who had to do much that is now done with the help of machinery. The strain was not always unrecognised, for the Minster workmen were allowed a period of rest during the working day.

Some of the men engaged in the construction of the Minster were not York men. The men employed there were by exception under ecclesiastical control. They were not governed by any of the city trade guilds. The master-mason was in charge of the whole of the building operations.

A list of trades in the city will suggest the kinds of business there were. Some of the names will go far to explain some modern surnames.

Wool Trades:—Mercers, Tapiters and Couchers (makers of tapestry, hangings, carpets, and coverlets), Fullers, Cardmakers, Littesters (dyers, listers), Shermen (shearmen), Sledmen, Dyers, Weavers of woollen.

Leather Trades:—Barkers (tanners), Curriers.

---

1. Cf. French *journee*.

Building Trades:—Carpenters, Wrights, Joiners, Plasterers, Tilers, Ironmongers, Painters, Glaziers.

Food Trades:—Spicers (grocers—*Cf.* French *epicier*), Cooks and waterleaders, Baxters (bakers), Vintners and taverners, Bouchers (butchers), Pulters (poultry-dealers), Wine-drawers (carters of wine), Sauce-makers.[1]

Outfitting Trades:—Tailors, Skinners (vestment makers), Glovers, Hosiers, Hatmakers, Capmakers, Cordwainers (cobblers), Saddlers, Girdlers and nailers, Spuriers and lorimers (makers of spurs, bits for bridles, etc.).

Armour Trades:—Armourers, Smiths, Bowers and flecchers (fletchers)—(makers of bows and arrows. *Cf,* French *fleche*).

Household Trades:—Coopers, Pewterers and founders, Chaundlers (makers of candles and wax images), Potters, Culters, Bucklemakers, sheathers, bladesmiths, Drapers, Linenweavers.

Miscellaneous Trades:—Goldsmiths, Latoners (workers in the metal called latten), Barber-surgeons (the mediaeval medical practitioners), Parchemeners and bookbinders, Scriveners, Writers of texts, Ostlers (inn-holders), Shipwrights, Fishers and mariners.

Artist craftsmen of York supplied most of the churches of the north of England with their beautiful vessels, furniture, and ornaments. In the workshops of the city, the metropolis of the north, there were worked and made embroidered vestments of all kinds, engraved chalices and vessels of silver and of gold, and carved work, including statues and images in stone, wood, and wax. Bells were cast with beautiful lettering. Brasses for grave-slabs were made bearing finely designed effigies.

Marketing, i.e., trading, was done mostly at the frequent and regular markets and at the fairs. The right to hold a market or a fair was among the rights obtained by means of royal charters. While markets were held once or several times a week or every day, fairs took place more rarely and at some of the most important and popular holiday seasons of the

---

1. Sauce was much used. The people of the Middle Ages had an especial liking for spices and highly-seasoned foods.

Business Life

year, like Whitsuntide. Fairs attracted a much larger public than the markets.

In the city there were markets in different places for different kinds of produce on certain days. For instance, in the fifteenth century there was a market of live-stock at Toft Green every Friday. The public squares, called Thursday Market and Pavement, were used as market-places. Some markets were held in the streets. Stalls were set up on which to exhibit the wares. The ordinary foodstuffs and materials, just as in the open market held at the present time in the long and broad Parliament Street, formed of Thursday Market and Pavement and the space formerly occupied by a compact mass of old houses between the two originally distinct squares, were the things sold and bought at the mediaeval markets: such as butter, meat, fish, linen, leather, corn, poultry, herbs. Some, for example butchers' shops, kept open market every day. Craftsmen worked goods at the premises of their merchant employers, which usually combined the latters' home and workshop; it was chiefly at the markets and fairs that these goods were sold.

Markets and fairs were controlled by the authority, whether municipal or archiepiscopal, that possessed the right of holding them. Again, particular care was taken to ensure preference being obtained by the citizens over strangers. The Lammas fairs were held under the authority of the Archbishops, who assumed the rule of the city and suburbs for the period of the fair. The sheriffs' authority, in consequence, was suspended for that period. The Archbishop, meanwhile, took tolls, and all cases that arose during the holding of the fair were judged by a court set up by him.

Fairs combined both trading and entertainments, for they were held on public holidays. They fostered trade and served to provide a change from the ordinary routine of life. It was perhaps at fairs that mediaeval people were at their noisiest, for these were occasions when they gave themselves up unrestrainedly to merry-making, wild and clamorous. Strolling players and the whole variety of mediaeval entertainers set up their stands and booths, and amused the dense surging crowds that thronged the squares and streets.

York had a large overseas trade, especially in wool and manufactured cloth. Some of its merchants owned property abroad. Some went abroad and encountered perils by sea and perils from foreigners on the continent. York traded with the Low Countries, where Veere (near Middleburg) and Dordrecht were ports that ships entered to discharge cargoes loaded on the York quays. The trade between York and the Baltic ports was much greater than that done with them from any other English port.

Foreign sailors were to be seen in the streets of fifteenth-century York; foreign goods were handled in the city. Wines were imported from France, fine cloths from Flemish towns, silks, velvet, and glass from Italy, while from the Baltic came timber and fur. From the North sea came fish, much of which was brought to York from the coast by packhorse across the moors. The herring was an important article of food.

Money was measured in marks, shillings, and pence. Of the current coins those in gold were called the angel, half-angel, the noble, half-noble, and quarter-noble; in silver there were the groat, half-groat, the penny, and half-penny. The local branch of the royal Mint was housed within the Castle. The building containing it was rebuilt in accordance with an order of 1423. The coins from this mint, which was at work during a large part of the fifteenth century, bore distinctive marks to show the place of minting. Silver coins bore the inscription CIVITAS EBORACI. The archbishops continued to use their privilege of coining money.

The following extracts, interesting for the substance and the literary form, are taken from the city records as published by the Surtees Society, vols. 120, 125, "The York Memorandum Book."

From the ordinances of the Pewterers, 1416.

"Ordinaciones pewderariorum.

"Ceux sont les articles de lez pewderers de Lounders, les queux les genz de mesme lartifice dyceste citee Deverwyk ount agrees pur agarder et ordeiner entre eux par deux ans passez, devant Johan Moreton, maire."

Others of the earlier ordinances are in Anglo-French; many are in Latin. Later ordinances are in English as in the case of those of the Carpenters, 1482, of which the following are the opening paragraphs:—

"In the honour of God, and for the weile of this full honourabill cite of York, and of the carpenters inhabit in the same at the special instaunce and praier of" . . . (here follows a list of names) . . . "carpenters of this full nobill cite, ar ordeyned the xxij^ti day of Novembyr in the xxij^ti yere of the reing of king Edward the iv. in the secund tym of the mairalte of the ryght honorabill Richard York mair of the said cite, by the authorite of the holl counsell of the said full honourable cite, for ewyr to be kept thez ordinaunces filluyg,

"Furst, for asmoch as here afore ther hath beyn of old tym a broderhode had and usyd emong the occupacion and craft above said, the wich of long continuaunce have usid, and as yit yerly usis to fynd of thar propir costes a lyght of diwyrs torchis in the fest of Corpus Christi day, or of the morn aftir, in the honour and worship of God and all saintes, and to go in procession with the same torchis with the blessid sacrament from the abbey foundyd of the Holy Trenite in Mykylgate in the said cite on to the cathedrall chyrch of Saint Petir in the same cite; and also have done and usyd diwyrs odir right full good and honourabill deides, as her aftir it shall more playnly apeir. It is ordenyd and esyablyshid be the said mair, aldermen, and all the holl counsell of the said full nobill cite, be the consent and assent of all tham of the said occupacion in the said cite, that the said fraternite and bredirhode shalbe here after for ewyr kept and continend as it has beyn in tymis passid, and that every brodir thar of shall pay yerly for the sustentacion thar of vjd, that is to say, at every halff yer iij^d, providyng allway that every man of the said occupacion within the said cite shalnot be compellid ne boundeyn to be of the said fraternite ne brodirhood, ne noyn to be thar of bot soch as will of thar free will."

Religious Life

Insistence can hardly be too great on the tremendous and widespread influence of the Church in the Middle Ages. The greatness of the Church continued during the fifteenth century; it derived from the traditions of an age when absolute power prevailed, from the undisputed usage of centuries, from a logical system of dogmas, and from international sanctions. The ornate services, allegiance to the distant Pope, the immense hold of the priests on the laity, the large territorial possessions of ecclesiastical bodies, impressed the people with the power of the

Church. These things came to the fifteenth century as established facts. The spirit of revolt indeed had appeared with Wiclif and his followers in the fourteenth century, but Lollardy met with severe repressive opposition. It was not till Tudor times that the new spirit, stimulated by the Revival of Learning, the Reformation, the invention of printing from type, geographical discovery, the suppression of long years of internecine warfare, and the establishment of a strong government, had accumulated enough energy to burst the bonds of mediaevalism. The fifteenth century was at the end of an age.

It is interesting to note that Wiclif (*d.* 1384), one of England's greatest men, was ordained in York. He stands out as a "daring and inspired pioneer" who strove to provide the land with priests who were true and earnest shepherds. He attempted the superhuman task of reviving true religion among a people that had become to a certain extent dull, irreverent, ignorant, and thoroughly superstitious.

By the fifteenth century the Church was suffering from those ills which needed and later gained drastic treatment. The Church had done almost miraculous work in the first few centuries of its existence, if we think only of the success with which it substituted its system of morality for that of pagan Rome. The fifteenth century followed those centuries when the Church of England, under the direction of great and earnest men, was doing its work with conspicuous success. Yet, the very forces that enabled the Church to make itself a living power in the Dark Ages, the early centuries embracing the Fall of Rome, the Empire of Charlemagne, and the kingship of Alfred the Great, became harmful to its continued activity beneficially in many directions. The inadequacy of its work in these centuries appears in the lack of spiritual activity and in the predominance of the material side of religion. The mediaeval Church suffered badly from excessive conservatism, which led towards sloth and a complacent inactivity. The morbid element showed itself during the fifteenth century mainly in lack of real earnestness, in the enjoyment of luxurious laziness, and in the steady neglect of the age to revise its Christianity. The Church moreover, with its complete segregation from other estates of the realm had become unpopular socially, while in its political and temporal aspects it had become an immense corporation with strong vested interests. Kings found it necessary to fight it; religious reformers had to rise up and overcome every form of repression used against them. The decadence is exemplified incidentally in the increasing poverty in material and expression of the monastic chronicles, which practically died out by 1485. The period of turmoil and change was yet to come.

Such was the general state of affairs. Nevertheless the forms and practices of the Church continued. The granting of indulgences and pardons, the inexhaustible demand for Peter's pence, went on vigorously. A recognised means of publicly raising funds was employed in February 1455–6, when the Archbishop proclaimed an indulgence of forty days to those who would help the Friars Preachers, whose cloister and buildings including 34 cells together with their books, vestments, jewels, and sacred vessels, had been destroyed by fire.

The faith of the ordinary citizen was, however, intact. The Church came into the people's life daily. The citizen could not walk away from his home without seeing a church, and meeting a priest or a friar. He attended the Church services and fulfilled his religious duties. Baptism, marriage, death, illness, public rejoicing, soldiering, dramatic entertainments, the language of daily life—all these bore the stamp of the Church. The very days of relief from work were holy-days, feast days in the Church's calendar. Taking part in the public processions on Corpus Christi Day, a great annual holiday, was a religious exercise; at the same time this day was devoted especially to entertainment. Wills of the century show that the citizens lived as religiously as formerly. This spirit is seen perhaps most characteristically in the numbers of candles that wealthy citizens bequeathed for use in church, and in the sums of money they left to specified clergy and other "religious" for the provision of masses for the souls of themselves, their wives and families, and for those for whom they ought to pray. Masses were thus provided for by hundreds, and in some cases by thousands. The following extracts from the will[1] of a rich citizen and merchant of York, who had been sheriff

---

1. As translated from the Latin by the late Mr. R.B. Cook and found among his valuable contributions to the publications of The Yorkshire Architectural Society.

and mayor of the city, show admirably the spirit of a member of the middle class in the fifteenth century:—

"In the name of God Amen. The 4th day of September in the year of our Lord 1436, I Thomas Bracebrig, Citizen and merchant, York, sound of mind and having health of body, establish and dispose my Will in this manner. First, I command and bequeath my soul to God Almighty, to the blessed Mary, Mother of God and ever Virgin, and to All Saints, and my body to be buried in the parish church of St. Saviour in York, before the image of the Crucifix of our Lord Jesus Christ, next to the bodies of my wives and children lately buried there, for having which burial in that place I bequeath to the fabric of the same parish church 20s. Also I bequeath for my mortuary my best garment with hood appropriate for my body. Also I bequeath to Master John Amall, Rector of the said parish church for my tithes and oblations forgotten, and that he may more specially pray for my soul, 20s. Also I bequeath for two candles to burn at my exequies 30 lbs. of wax. Also 10 torches to burn around my body on the said day of my burial, and that each torch shall contain in itself 14 lbs. of pure wax. . . . Also I bequeath to 10 men carrying or holding the said 10 Torches in my exequies 10 Gowns, so that each of the said 10 poor men shall have in his gown and hood 3–1/2 ells of russet or black cloth, and that the aforesaid gowns shall be lined with white woollen cloth. And I will that my Executors shall pay for the making of the same gowns with hoods. . . . Also I will and ordain that two fit and proper chaplains shall be found to celebrate for my soul, and the souls of my parents, wives, children, benefactors, and for the souls of those for whom I am bound or am debtor, as God shall know in that respect, and for the souls of all the faithful departed, for one whole year, immediately after my decease, in my parish church. . . ."

The will is a very long one. Altogether 470 lbs. of wax, to last 15 years, would be necessary to satisfy the requirements of the will. 765 masses are specially arranged for; besides, provision was made for masses to be said by more than 21 chaplains, the religious of 5 priories for women, and by every friar and priest of the four orders of friars in York. There were also bequests to 2 anchoresses, 1 anchorite, and 1 hermit, to pray for the soul of the testator and the souls aforesaid. Bequests were made to the poor of St. Saviour's; to lepers "in the 4 houses for lepers in the suburbs," to the poor in maisons-dieu; to the prisoners in the Castle, in the Archbishop's prison, and in the Kidcote. The testator ordered gifts of coal, wood, and shoes, and 1000 white loaves of bread, to be made among the poor and needy. The bequests to relatives and directions to the Executors occupy a large part of the Will, which is that of a particularly wealthy and important citizen. Charity, however, was a marked characteristic of these men who had become rich through trade. With a generous spirit they put into practice the teachings about giving to the poor and to prisoners. The amount of money spent in founding chantries, in paying priests for masses for the departed, testifies to their faith.

It was part of the policy of the Church to keep the instruction of the people, young and old, in its own control. Practically all the educational work in York during the century was the work of the Church.

Through the monasteries and hospitals the Church did valuable work in feeding the poor, helping the needy, and in educating the poorer citizens' boys. The royal Hospital of St. Leonard did such work. It was a peculiar institution, being under the authority of the King, and containing a sisterhood as well as a brotherhood. It included a grammar school and a song-school. As an institution it was self-supporting; food was made on the premises, and the carpenters' and similar work was done by brethren in the Hospital's own workshops.

The large number of priests were variously employed. There were priests who officiated in the monastic churches, in the parish churches (as rectors and chaplains, of whom there were 300 in York in 1436), in the cathedral where the number of chantry-chapels was very great and where services were held simultaneously as well as frequently. Some priests were vicars, that is, while the living or "cure" of souls was held by the rector, the vicar was the actual priest in charge, for the rector probably held more than one benefice and could not serve personally in more than one. Generally it was a corporate body, like the Dean and Chapter, or a monastery, that was the rector of a number of livings at the same time.

Of the many clergy serving the Minster the Dean, who was the incumbent, ranked first. Much of the revenue of the Dean and Chapter, the Governing Body, came from landed possessions in York and various parts of the surrounding country. These possessions, divided into prebends, provided livings for the thirty-six prebendaries or canons, who collectively formed the Chapter. Each canon served at the Minster during a specified portion of the year, when he lived at his residence at York. The residences of the prebendaries were mostly round the Minster Close. While his own parish was served vicariously while he was at York, each canon had a minor-canon or vicar-choral to act as his deputy at York when he was absent. These vicars-choral formed a corporate body and lived collegiately in the Bedern. The numerous chantries in the Minster were served by priests who also lived collegiately but at St. William's College. The College, at the head of which was a Provost, was founded about the middle of the century. Previously these priests had lived in private houses.

The parish priest was occupied in performing the services in his church, in hearing confessions, in teaching the children, in visiting, interrogating, consoling, and ministering the Sacraments to the sick and dying, and in guiding and sharing the life of his parish generally. Each parish church had a number of clergy besides the parish priest attached to it: the number varied from one to ten or more according to the number of chantries at the church. Each priest was helped a great deal in parochial affairs by the parish clerk. The latter was the chief lay official for business in connection with the parish church. His duties required him to be a man of some education.

The Archbishop was both bishop of the diocese of York, and head of all the dioceses which together formed the Northern Province of the two provinces into which England was divided for the purpose of Church rule. His diocese formerly extended so far south as to include Nottingham and Southwell.

The Archbishop was a Primate and occupied a high position in the State. Besides being supreme head of the Church in the northern province, he was a great landowner. He possessed, besides his palace near the Minster, a number of seats (like Cawood Castle) in the country. When he was in London he resided at his fine official palace, York House. The Archbishops were great lords of the realm in every way. Archbishop Neville, brother of Warwick "the king-maker," celebrated his installation in 1465 with a very famous feast. The huge amount and delicacy of the

Religious Life

dishes prepared, the number of retainers employed, the splendour of the scene, which was honoured by the presence of the Duke of Gloucester and members of some of the most noble families in the kingdom, all the details of this sumptuous feast, were intended to impress King Edward IV with the might of the Nevilles.

Ecclesiastical preferment was often a reward for services in other branches of the service of the State. Sometimes great offices in the Church and the State were held simultaneously. Thus, Archbishop Rotherham was also Chancellor of England for a time. Both Richard Scrope and William Booth, archbishops of the century, had been lawyers. The appointment of George Neville, who had been nominated when only twenty-three to the see of Exeter, was a purely political one, the bestowing of a high and lucrative office on a member of a noble family that was enjoying the full sunshine of popularity and power. The King could also benefit from Church positions otherwise than by presenting them to partisans. During the two and a half years that the see of York was kept vacant between the time of the execution of Archbishop Scrope and the appointment of Henry Bowett (in 1407), the revenues went, in accordance with the established practice, to the royal purse.

There were also "clerks," educated men, but not priests, who were in "minor orders." Many a man, asserting that he was a clerk, made application for trial by an ecclesiastical court, so as to get the benefit of the less stringent judgment of the Church courts, to which belonged the right of dealing with ecclesiastical offenders.

One abuse within the Church was pluralism, that is, the holding of more than one office at the same time with the result that the holder was drawing revenue for work he could not himself do. William Sever, for instance, while Abbot of St. Mary's, York, became Bishop of Carlisle. These two high offices, one monastic and the other secular, he held simultaneously from 1495 to 1502.

The religious orders were of two kinds, viz. monks (and nuns) who lived in seclusion in monasteries, abbeys, or convents, and friars, who lived under a rule but came out into the world to preach and work. Both kinds took the vows of chastity, poverty, and obedience to the rule (*e.g.,* Cistercian or Benedictine, Franciscan or Dominican). Some, but not all, monks and friars were priests. There were four well-known orders of mendicant friars, viz. Franciscan (Grey friars, friars minor), Dominican (Black friars, friars preachers), Carmelite (White friars), Augustinian (Austin canons). Monks and friars wore sandals, and long, loose gowns with hoods or cowls which they could pull over their heads to serve as hats. The alternative titles of some of the orders of friars came from the colour of their friars' gowns. The Carmelites used undyed cloth, which was white in comparison with the black of the Dominicans. The Benedictine monks of St. Mary's Abbey wore black garments. Their heads were shaved on the crown, the technical term for which was the tonsure.

Monks spent their time in attending the frequent services in the monastery church, which they entered at the night and early morning services directly from the dormitories; in copying manuscripts, which occupied a large part of their day; in contemplation and in study; in manual work; in recreation. The cloister where work was carried on and the church were the essential buildings of the monastery. Monastic life centred in these two places. Its arrangements were dictated by the purpose of making a religious atmosphere pervade everything; thus a religious book was read at meals.

The luxury and laxity that obtained in monastic life were not confined to the fifteenth century. The Archbishop had frequent occasion in the fourteenth century to complain, for instance, of the use by monks and nuns of ornaments, and of clothes of finer material than the traditional rule permitted. He condemned the wearing of clothes cut to a worldly pattern. The religious had to be admonished from time to time not to admit strangers within the cloister, and to conform in all respects strictly to their rule.

During the century St. Mary's Abbey contained about sixty monks, including the Abbot, the supreme head, and the Prior, who held the second highest office; besides, there was a very large number of lay-brethren, servants and officers, for in addition to the internal work at the abbey, there was the management of the abbey estates and business. Abbots and monks were always keen traders. Altogether the personnel of St. Mary's might have numbered about two hundred.

The influence of such a monastery as St. Mary's was very far from being restricted to affairs within the abbey walls. Through its Abbot it had a spokesman in the House of Lords. There were cells dependant on the abbey and often at a distance. The Abbot had a number of residences in the country and one in London. The abbey itself had numerous possessions of land and manors in many parts of the country. This was a principal source of revenue. St. Mary's Abbey also had jurisdiction over many churches, not only in York and Yorkshire, but in other counties as well. The other monastic institutions and the Minster and some of the hospitals, for example St. Leonard's, had similar rights of jurisdiction and the ownership of land, property, and churches.

In some of the churchyards there lived anchorites, anchoresses, and hermits. These were individuals who chose to live a solitary life spent in prayer and religious work. Anchorites led a life of strict seclusion, for they were literally shut in their cells, from the world. They did not, however, eschew all intercourse with others, for their solitary lives of devotion, and in some cases of study, gave them a reputation for wisdom that led people to seek them for their advice. Permission was given by the Church authorities to those who took up this mode of life, the assumption of which formed part of a special service. The Pontifical of Archbishop Bainbridge, who held the see from 1508 to 1514, contains an office for the Enclosing of an Anchorite. Hermits lived in less strict seclusion. Their aims were similar, but they went about in the world doing good works.

One of the worst features of the religious decadence of the Middle Ages was the craftiness of such spurious types of men as those whom Chaucer painted in the Pardoner and the Somonour, and Charles Reade depicted in the peripatetic "cripples" of "The Cloister and the Hearth." Chaucer wrote in the true spirit of comedy *mores corrigere ridendo,* but Langland, his contemporary, who described similar types of men of State as well as of Church, did so from the point of view of a moral reformer whose satire is a trenchant weapon.

There were many other types of religious men, but it must suffice to refer to Pardoners, who by virtue of papal bulls gave pardons, expecting, exacting if necessary, a reward in return, and to mention only palmers and pilgrims, who were seen in York when they came to visit the shrine of St. William in the Minster. The palmers were pilgrims who had visited the Holy Land. They liked to wear a scallop-shell in their broad-brimmed hats as a sign of their extensive travels. Journeying from shrine to shrine was a favourite occupation, a professional one, of those pilgrims who loved a wandering and easy life, seeing the sights and living at the expense of the monastic hospitality. Some pilgrimages were done by proxy, through the employment of professional pilgrims. A pilgrimage to a shrine celebrated for miraculous cures or the efficacy of the spiritual benefit derived from worshipping at it and invoking the help of the saint, was for many an exercise of deep religious devotion. There is no doubt, moreover, that at the shrines of the saints the Church proved itself a great healer. It was in fact the popular physician. Apart from surgery, the medical practice of the twentieth century is in some ways the successor of that of the Church of the fifteenth.

When very popular religious men died, or when, if they were already dead as in the case of William, Archbishop of York (who died in 1153 and was canonised in 1227), popularity sprang up, it was quite usual for it to be discovered that miracles were being wrought at their tombs. The case of the popular Archbishop Scrape who was executed is a typical one. In this way the calendar of saints was enlarged, the devout had a new interest, the Church maintained its position in the popular eye and mind, and its funds increased.

The mediaeval Church, however, appeared perhaps at its best in its Church services, which drew their effect from the sanctity of the magnificent building (whether cathedral or parish church), the awe inspired by the Church politic, the use of Latin and the learned atmosphere, the religious teaching, and, not least, the imposing ceremonies, and the ornate ritual performed amid a profusion of lighted wax candles by priests and dignitaries in resplendent vestments.

Education

The only school engaged in higher education in York in the century was St. Peter's School, a very old foundation, where Alcuin, who (in 782) had carried educational reform to the land of the Franks, had been master. At this school, which was attached to the cathedral, were educated those who were to spend their lives in scholarship, especially, as now, after residence at Oxford or Cambridge; future priests and clerks; the sons of the nobility and of the more wealthy members of the mer-

Education

chant class in the city. Other regular schools were the Grammar School at the royal Hospital of St. Leonard and the one at Fossgate Hospital. This educational work was one of the most valuable kinds of public work done by these hospitals.

A more elementary and less well organised education was given by the parish priests and the chantry priests, from whom the children of the city generally, boys and girls, received at least oral instruction.

Girls usually received a practical upbringing at home. The only schools for girls were those attached to women's monasteries, of which there was St. Clement's Nunnery alone in York.

Educational welfare work, as distinct from direct and organised class-teaching, was carried on by the friars, the religious men who lived under a rule but who went out to work in the world, instead of spending their lives in seclusion as the monks did. The Dominican and Franciscan Friars played an important part in education by teaching, especially at the Universities. Education was also a foremost interest of the Augustinians, who supported a college at Oxford.

Books, which had all to be written by hand, were scarce. The copying of manuscripts, which was done mostly in the monasteries, was laborious work. Instruction was given as a rule orally, but also by means of pictorial art and drama. The stained-glass windows were more than ornamental additions to the church building: they were part of the means of instruction. Mediaeval drama had originated in the Church's effort to make events described in the gospel more real through their representation dramatically.

The teaching of manual skill and craftsmanship was entirely the work of the masters of the crafts under the general supervision of the guilds. The work of the age was made beautiful, and being handwork each piece of work gained the interest of individuality. The details of architectural ornament, in consequence, show wonderful diversity of form. The naive spirit of the ordinary handicraft workman was often reflected in his work. The arts of the goldsmith, silversmith, bell-founder, vestment-maker (which required elaborate embroidery), and the sculptor, were practised in York with excellent results.

There has never been a university of York, although under Alcuin the school of York was doing work of high quality, work that gained European fame. Even within the last hundred years, when so many provincial universities and university colleges have been established, York, one of the most appropriate places, has not obtained a university.

News and information reached the citizens mainly from personal intercourse. Merchants visiting other cities discussed with fellow merchants not only their immediate business but also past and current events. Pilgrims, palmers, and sailors recited their adventures on distant seas and lands, and told of the wonders of the world. The ordinary citizen, who read little, depended on conversations with better-informed citizens and strangers. The city council was continually in communication with the King and the great officers of State: information filtered down from the council to the citizens. The messengers often supplied the latest semi-official news. Officials and servants attached to the royal service or to that of nobles or of ecclesiastics (like the Archbishop of York), were the source of much political gossip. The news of the country passed to and fro between the city and the monastic lands, the castles, the manors, and the forests by means of the visits of men who lived at those places. Markets and fairs and public assemblies, whether the holding of assizes or on State visits, were occasions for the dissemination of news. The ordinary citizen gathered news and information also from the pulpit and from guild and parochial meetings, and from the bellman. The only authoritative news he received at first hand he got by listening to the public reading of proclamations.

In the Middle Ages educated men who had no inclination for the life of the Church, monastic or secular, nor for landed proprietorship, with which was combined hunting and soldiering, became clerks. The clerks in the royal service helped in the work of administration of national affairs. Tradesmen's sons of ability and opportunity succeeded in gaining good positions in this service. Nobles also employed clerks.

Altogether there seems to have been in the fifteenth century good provision for higher education. The people of the Middle Ages were not illiterate. The outstanding age of illiteracy (not to mention a host of other evils) in England was the age that began with the Industrial Revolution, when statesmen failed to make the public services keep pace with the rapidly increasing population and the rapid development of new conditions. That there was as large a public ready and eager to buy the books that printing from type made possible has been regarded as a disproof of general illiteracy. The books were published in the vernacular: the people read them. It was in 1476 that Caxton set up his press at Westminster. The first printing press established in York was set up in 1509.

Nevertheless the general state of education and scholarship in England in the fifteenth century was at a low level, mainly owing to lack of enthusiasm and to the limited subjects of study. Natural science was unable yet to flourish. Mediaeval education was humanistic, but the old springs of this form of study were nearly dried up. The Greek classics were entirely lost. Even the few Latin classics that the mediaevals possessed, they did not understand aright. To Virgil's AEneid they gave a Christian interpretation! Grammar was the basis of study, which dealt mainly with such works as those of Cicero, Virgil, Boethius.

The fifteenth century, the last century of an age, was a backwater in education as in literature. The great revival was to come. The fifteenth century was indeed a century of revolution in so far as under the almost placid surface of continuity and conformity, there were forces of revolt at work, probing, accumulating knowledge and experience, perhaps unconsciously, for the day of liberation and change. The Bible was not yet popularly available. Wiclif had been a pioneer in the work of translation and publication, but Tyndale and Coverdale in the sixteenth century supplied what he had aimed at doing in the fourteenth. The fifteenth century was the quiet dark hour before the dawn. As Coleridge expressed it: No sooner had the Revival of learning "sounded through Europe like the blast of an archangel's trumpet than from king to peasant there arose an enthusiasm for knowledge, the discovery of a manuscript became the subject of an embassy: Erasmus read by moonlight because he could not afford a torch, and begged a penny, not for the love of charity, but for the love of learning." But even then, when the enthusiasm and the will were there, such was the dearth of material for learning that, as in the case of Erasmus, the pioneers had practically nothing to work at but the classical texts and a few meagre vocabularies with etymologies of mediaeval scholarship. In 1491 Grocyn began to teach Greek at Oxford. In 1499 Erasmus first visited England. Referring to his visit to this country in 1505–6 he wrote: "There are in London five or six men who are thorough masters of both Latin and Greek; even in Italy I doubt that you would find their equals." England's position was, therefore, in this respect a good one.

Entertainments

In the Middle Ages holidays were taken at festivals marked in the Church calendar. Some feasts, like that of Whitsuntide, were universally observed. The ordinary length of a festival was eight days, that is, the full week—the octave. Apart from pilgrimages, the ordinary people travelled little. Moreover the life and property of travellers were not altogether secure in the forest land, with the result that treasure and distinguished people travelled under the care of an armed escort. A large city like York was practically self-supporting in public amusements. The fifteenth century saw the full development of the religious mystery plays, and the allegorical morality plays, which with their comic interludes had become popular from the thirteenth and fourteenth centuries. The feast of Corpus Christi (instituted about 1263) was the most important time in the year for the playing of these typically mediaeval dramas. Begun more than three centuries earlier within the Church and performed by the clergy, as a dramatic reinforcement of the services and preaching, the mediaeval drama owed its origin mainly to the Church which maintained its influence as long as this drama continued. It soon came into the care of laymen, who took part in the productions. In the fifteenth century, these plays, which were produced almost entirely by laymen, were so numerous that they were formed in cycles or groups. The texts of some of the most famous cycles, those of York, Chester, Wakefield, and Coventry, have survived. The various trade-guilds made themselves responsible for the production of one pageant of the local cycle, or two or three guilds joined to produce a pageant, so that the whole city produced a large number of plays to celebrate the feast of Corpus Christi. Among its officers a guild had its pageant-master, whose duty it was to supervise the guild's dramatic work.

Entertainments

The York plays, the texts dating from the middle of the fourteenth century, are extant. In 1415 fifty-seven pageant plays were produced. Productions were made in York down to 1579. The following are examples taken from among the fifty-seven plays and guilds:—

The Shipwrights produced the Building of the Ark,
the Fishers and Mariners produced Noah and the Flood,
the Spicers produced the Annunciation,
the Tilers produced the Birth of Christ,
the Goldsmiths produced the Adoration,
the Vintners produced the Wedding in Cana,
the Skinners produced the entry into Jerusalem,
the Baxters produced the Last Supper,
the Tapiters and Couchers produced the Christ before Pilate,
the Saucemakers produced the Death of Judas,
the Bouchers produced the Death of Christ,
the Carpenters produced the Resurrection,
the Scriveners produced the Incredulity of Thomas,
the Tailors produced the Ascension,
the Mercers produced the Day of Judgment.

The full cycle gave in dramatic form the leading episodes of the Scriptures from the Creation to the Last Day.

While the trade-guilds were thus responsible for individual pageants, help and control were given by the Guild of Corpus Christi (inaugurated in 1408 and incorporated in 1459), and the city council. The guild had a very large number of members, among whom were the Archbishop, many bishops and abbots and nobles. These dramatic productions belonged to the religious and social sides of the guilds. The plays, however, did not always provoke pleasure, for sometimes members of some of the guilds complained of the financial burden they were forced to bear in order to produce the plays allotted to them.

The guilds also took part in public processions with torches on Corpus Christi Day in celebration of this popular festival. In the processions, which were closely connected with the religious and guild-phases of city life, there walked city clergy wearing their surplices, the master of the Guild of Corpus Christi, the guild officials, the bearers of the shrine of the guild, the mayor, aldermen and corporation, and officers and members of the Guild of Corpus Christi and of the city trade-guilds. As the procession went on its way litanies and chants were sung by the clergy. The shrine, the central feature of the procession, was presented in 1449. It was itself of gilt and had many images some of which were gilded, while the main ones under the "steeple" were in mother-of-pearl, silver, and gold: to it were attached rings, brooches, girdles, buckles, beads, gawds and crucifixes, in gold and silver, and adorned with coral and jewels.

On the occasion of the processions and performances of pageants, as at fairs, the city was filled with a boisterous multitude which turned what was by tradition a religious exercise and entertainment, to a time of riotous merry-making, and uncouth disorder. In 1426 a kind of crusade was preached by a friar minor, William Melton, against the riotous and drunken conduct of the people at the Corpus Christi festival. He denounced the disgracing of the festival and affirmed that the people were forfeiting by their conduct the indulgences granted for the festival. The result of the friar's crusade was the holding of a special meeting of the city council, which decided that the processions and pageants were to be held on separate days, the pageants on the eve of Corpus Christi, and the procession on the feast itself. Formerly both had taken place on the same day.

The pageants were produced in suitable parts of the city. Stages on wheels were brought to these places, some of them open spaces, others main streets. The stages, which were the work of citizen workmen, were of three storeys, the central and principal one, the stage proper, representing the earth. Demons, in gaudy attire, came up from the flame-region of the lowest storey; divine messengers and personages came down from the star and cloud adorned tipper storey. The tiring-room was below and behind the stage. The acting was by members of the guilds. They, no doubt, practised here, as elsewhere, the ranting delivery of their speeches so denounced by Hamlet in his critical address to the Players, whom he admonished to speak "trippingly on the tongue" and not to "out-Herod Herod." There are several references in Shakespeare to these plays of the Middle Ages. For instance, in *Twelfth Night*:

"Like to the old Vice . . .
Who with dagger of lath
In his rage and his wrath,
Cries, Ah, ah! to the devil."

and in *Henry V:*

". . . this roaring devil i' the old play
that every one may pare his nails with a wooden dagger."

Stands for spectators were erected by private enterprise for profit in many places in the city. The general assembly, preparatory to the beginning of the performances, took place on Pageant Green, now called Toft Green (which lies behind that side of Micklegate which is opposite Holy Trinity). The first performances were made at the gates of Holy Trinity Priory (on the west side of the river); there were four performances in Micklegate (a street near the Priory); four in Coney Street (the main street on the east side of the river)—and likewise performances in other parts of the city. The last three performances took place at the gates of the Minster; in Low Petergate, and in Pavement, which was one of the city market squares.

When Richard III came to York in 1483, part of his entertainment consisted of performances of pageants.

The only other public dramatic entertainments were crude, coarse, popular plays, done by strolling players. A mediaeval crowd at fair time was entertained by mountebanks, tumblers, and similar rough makers of unrefined mirth.

The Corporation had a band of minstrels in its service.

Of physical games archery was the most practised. This was the national physical exercise, one which had helped the English soldiers to gain a great reputation for themselves, as at Agincourt (1415). At York the "butts," where men practised archery, were outside the city walls.

Classes

Class divisions were well marked. They appeared in manners, in dress, and in occupation.

Fashions varied considerably as the century progressed. There were close-fitting dresses and loose ones, small head-dresses like the caul (a jewelled net to bind in the hair) and high and broad erections that went to the other extreme. Men now wore their hair long; later they had it close-cropped. Perhaps the most wonderful fashion was that which men followed in wearing hose of different colours. With all the vagaries of fashion the most striking feature of dress was the use of rich and a manifold variety of colours. Excepting the case of the dress of the religious, which was generally of a sombre hue, colour characterised men's clothes as much as it did the dresses of women. The doublet was the coat of the time. Sleeves were generally big. Long and pointed shoes were characteristic, but it was the cloak that proved so effective a piece of dress, the cloak that has such scenic possibilities, that can so nicely express character. There were only few kinds of personal ornament. The most usual were brooches, belts, chains, and pendants, and especially finger-rings, of which the signet ring was a popular form.

The nobles, great landowners, in many cases of Norman origin, were lords over a considerable number of people. York, being a royal city, escaped many of the troubles consequent on rule by an immediate overlord. Besides himself, his family, and personal servants, a lord provided for a retinue of armed retainers, who formed a kind of body-guard and a force to serve the king as occasion demanded; in addition, important household officials, such as secretaries and treasurers. Among noblemen's followers there were many dependents, some, no doubt, parasites, but a number, especially if literary men, in need of patronage to help them to live as well as to pursue their vocation.

The different kinds of religious men have already been mentioned from archbishops and abbots to the scurrilous impostors who used a religious exterior to rob poor people, at whose expense they lived well a wandering, loose, hypocritical life. In York, there were monks and friars, cathedral, parochial, and chantry priests, and clerks. The monastic life was a recognised profession. In the monasteries there were, besides regular monks, novices or those who aspired to take the full monastic vows, and, especially in the fifteenth century, by which time the importance of lowly, arduous service for the brethren and personal labour had lapsed, a very large number of semi-religious and lay brethren, who were really servants to the regular monks. In the fifteenth century the religious houses were extremely wealthy. Some of the monks were of noble birth. Nobles, when travelling, usually lodged at the monastic houses, which were dotted all over England. The kings resided often at abbeys when visiting the provinces. Richard III, when Duke of Gloucester, resided at the Austin Friary in York.

The one monastic house for women was St. Clement's Nunnery. There were, moreover, sisterhoods in the hospitals of, for example, St. Leonard and St. Nicholas.

St. Leonard's Hospital, among its many functions, was a home of royal pensioners.

The townspeople were chiefly merchants and tradesmen and those they employed, and the wives and families of all of them. Men of this type, both rich and poor, rose to important positions in trade and city life, and in the King's service. Some entered the service of nobles. Great dignity was attached to the higher positions of authority in city and guild life. Trade led to wealth and increased comfort and a higher social state. Men in the King's service received preferment more often than direct monetary reward.

Women had only the monastic life to enter as a profession. They could become full members of a number of the York trade-guilds. The social position of women in the retrograde fifteenth century fully agrees with the absence of women from among those who achieved notability in the city during the century.

The most interesting type of citizens was that composed of the freemen, who formed the vast majority of the inhabitants. As the name implies, they were historically the descendants of the men who in earlier times were freed from serfdom. It was the freemen who, through the Mayor and Corporation, paid rent to the King for the city, its rights and possessions. There are still, it may be noted, freemen of the city, distinct from those distinguished men who have received its honorary freedom. The main privileges of the mediaeval freemen included the right of trading in the city, and of voting. They also had rights over the common lands attached to the city, and they were eligible to fill the offices of local civic government if thought wealthy enough to be elected into such a "close self-elected corporation."

Everyday Life in the City

Soldiers of the royal army were stationed in York at the Castle. The Wars of the Roses, wars of kings and nobles, lasted from 1455 to 1485 and, although York itself hardly experienced the warfare, it saw contingents of the forces of both sides, as well as the leaders and royal heads of both parties.

There lived in the city a number of men in the royal service. Some worked at the administrative offices of the royal forest of Galtres, Davy Hall, where the chief officer himself dwelt. There were also the men who worked at the royal Fish Pond near which was Fishergate in which street most of these men lived.

Those afflicted with leprosy, a disease which in England disappeared toward the end of the fifteenth century, dwelt apart for fear of infecting the healthy. The four hospitals outside the four main entrances to the city served to keep the disease isolated.

York received from time to time a large number and a great diversity of visitors. Distinguished visitors usually received gifts from the Corporation. Kings, queens, and full court and retinue came, and sometimes the entire houses of Parliament. At such times great crowds of nobles, spiritual lords, commoners, officers, military and civil, thronged the city and taxed its accommodation. On such an occasion as Richard III's attendance at the Minster for mass, or the visit of Henry V, the narrow streets were packed to suffocation with people assembled to watch the processions of gorgeously arrayed sovereigns, princes, peers, ecclesiastics, soldiers, and distinguished commoners. The Duke of Gloucester, afterwards Richard III, was very popular in the North, especially in York, where he was received (as in 1483) with magnificence and festivity. The north was loyal to him and gave him much support in his political schemes.

The visits of the royal judges of assize, of sailors and pilgrims, have already been mentioned. Pedlars, who were active nomad tradesmen, were always to be found in town and country dealing in their small wares.

Last, and some of the unhappiest, among the types of people to be found in a mediaeval city were serfs who had absconded from the lands or the service to which they were bound. They sometimes fled to a city for the security it afforded. Serfdom, however, was rapidly disappearing.

Chapter 5

CONCLUSION

Life in York in the fifteenth century was active. Trade, home and continental, was flourishing. Building operations were in hand; work was always proceeding at the Minster or at one or other of the religious houses and churches. There were so many social elements established in and visiting York that something of interest was always taking place. Entertainments were plentiful and pageants were as well produced in York as anywhere in the kingdom. The city enjoyed a particularly large measure of local government. Its reputation was great. According to contemporary standards it was a fine prosperous city, one that contained resplendent ecclesiastical buildings that were second to none. In short, it was a "full nobill cite."

Although the present city looks, in parts, more typically mediaeval than modern, York today forms a very great contrast with the fifteenth-century city. We are separated from the fifteenth century by the Renaissance, the Reformation, and Tudor England, by the Civil War and the Restoration, by the "age of prose and reason," the keen-minded and rough-mannered eighteenth century, by the Industrial Revolution, and by that second Renaissance, the Victorian Age, during which the amenities of daily life were revolutionised. Radical changes are to be seen, for example, in the style of architecture, the mode of transmission of news, the methods of transport, the form of municipal government, the maintenance of the public peace, and in social relationships, more particularly with regard to industry and commerce and the parts played by employer and employed. The number of inhabitants today is about six

Conclusion

times that of the mediaeval city. The contrast, which is so great in most ways as to be quite obvious, is an interesting and profitable study, but it might have been founded on more precise data, for, great as is the amount of valuable material that York can supply concerning its history, investigation shows how much greater that amount would have been had the city and its rulers during the last century or two realised the value of the accumulated original historical riches that it contained.

Whereas the moderns obliterated practically all they came against, fortunately the earlier people were content to make no change beyond what was immediately necessary. Hence the survival of material most valuable to the historian and archaeologist. York, as it is today, is a city marvellously rich in survivals of past ages. It is also, as a result especially of the nineteenth century, a city of destruction. While we may regret but not repine at the disappearance of much of interest and value as the result of progress, yet wanton, ruthless destruction, such as has taken place within the last century, deserves the sternest denunciation. In spite of its being, in consequence, a "city of destruction," York is a store-house of original material for the history of England. Its records are in earth, stone, brick, wood, plaster, bone, and coin-metal; on parchment, paper, and glass; above the ground and below it—everywhere and in every form. This wealth of historical material, connected with practically every period of our national history, is a priceless possession and one that is not yet exhausted.

www.ingramcontent.com/pod-product-compliance
Lightning Source LLC
Chambersburg PA
CBHW031426040426
42444CB00006B/697